Conversations with My Guardian Angel

by

M.K. Sullivan

DAXSON PUBLISHING

Foreword

In so many situations, as children we are faced in having to deal with death at early ages. I lost my mother when I was five years old, and in dealing with such an empty space, I struggled to find peace in the midst of grief. M.K Sullivan's collection takes us on a journey in her own grief struggle. She lost her dad at thirteen years old, and through her poetry, she captures those complicated moments when grief hits you unexpectedly. As we grow up, and deal with life in our young adulthood the grief hits differently, but it is still present in our daily lives. As we hit our thirties, the loss is still very present even though the death happened years ago. This book is for every person who has lost a loved one and who still is often hit with grief in unexpected places. M.K. Sullivan's book shows us the true reality of grief and how as life continues, there are moments when grief knocks us to the ground, and at other times a few tears fall from our eyes, and all these moments are just reminders of how much we love and miss our loved one.

Erica Castro

Author of: *Finding Peace through the Grieving Process* and *The Pain Left Behind: Surviving a Suicide Loss*

Conversations with My Guardian Angel
© 2025 M.K. Sullivan
ISBN: 9781966337249
First Edition, 2025

Printed in the United States of America

Edited by: M.K. Sullivan

Cover Design by: Alejandra J. Lopez

Layout Design by: Erica Castro

I dedicate this chapbook to Bailey, Lilith, Aliza, Alejandra
and Peter, Erica and Daxson
Publishing, Lopez Urban Farm, and all who have supported
me along my grief journey
and allowed me to support them during theirs.
Let's grieve together.
xoxo,
MK

Table of Contents

Prologue

Part 1: Grief In Adolescence

2-15-10..17
After...18
Bad Romance..19
My Elevator Pitch.......................................20
An Inconvenient Truth...............................21
Call Waiting..22
Mount Comfort...23
The Dress Rehearsal...................................24
Charlie's Song...25
Wind up Toy..26
My Saturday Plans......................................27
The Ballad Of Allen Iverson.....................28
Telephone..30
Ouija, Are You There?................................31
Mixtape..32
Monster Protocol..33
Untitled Conversation with a Stranger at a Bonfire in the Middle of an Empty Field...................34
Player Stats: An Overview.........................35
Graduation (High School).........................36

Part 2: Grief in Early 20s

First Date...43
Wales Vs. Australia....................................44
Daddy Issues..45

An Ode to Father's Day...46

Déjà Vu..47

Graduation (Undergrad)...48

Part 3: Grief in Mid 20s

Missing Signal...55

Grief Journaling..56

Coming Out (pt. 1) 57

Graduation (Grad School) 58

D.D.C. 59

Health Update(2021)...60

Rehearsal Dinner 61

Hospital (Night One)..62

Putting Pen To Paper..63

Daffodils...64

PNES..65

Part 4: Grief in Late 20s

Coming Out (pt. 2)..71

Your Valentine...73

California (Night One)..74

The Novel..75

Words of Wisdom...76

Health Update (2025)..77

Fatherless Behavior 78

I Hate This Poem...79

Pacing..80

Epilogue..85

Conversations with My Guardian Angel

Prologue

I often believe that grief lives in our dreams. I dream about my father all the time. Some dreams feel so real; it's like I'm sitting in the room with him again. My father passed away suddenly in 2010. I was 13 years old. Other than the "five stages of grief" chart my guidance counselor showed me in her office, I had very little tools on how to navigate grief. I assumed grieving was a private and solitary experience. Over the years I began to experience loud and painful disruptions to my daily life. My unattended trauma was impacting my daily functioning. It was worsening my chronic illnesses. The externalized and internalized ableism I experienced as the result of my major life event has impacted me forever. I want to share my story and to help people grieve. We don't grieve alone. We never have. Reconnecting with myself and my disabled siblings has helped me understand how to navigate the world. Some days it's easy and some days I need help from my community.

Part 1: Grief In Adolescence

2-15-10

Dad,
It's only been one day.

How am I meant
                    to go on

 Without you
                by my side

After

What happens after we die?
I don't know every answer

But in some cases
There's a viewing two days after the autopsy
Don't worry we put an ad in the paper
and shared it on Facebook.
Often there's a lot of home cooked meals
From well-meaning neighbors
But mostly,
It's just empty sad looks
Because no one knows how to talk to you

Maybe this feeling will pass
After a while.

Bad Romance

We are sitting in car
on the far edge of the parking lot
The night sky is splattered
with dim stars
trapped behind a silver wave of clouds

No one moves
Maybe if we stay still
We don't have to go back inside
I can't go back near the casket

I hear the opening drums
Before anyone can open the car door, I shout
MY DAD LOVES THIS SONG
Auntie reaches for the volume dial
We scream and thrash our heads

Suddenly, everything is a blur
of laughter and music
I almost forget where we are
But then, the song ends.

My Elevator Pitch

I prepare my speech for the board
Maybe I'll start with my desire to see
More friends or maybe my need to catch up on home-
work
Or I can even make up some upcoming field trip!

Anything to get me out of this house of mourning
I'm drowning in my own grief.

I take a deep breath.

*"May I please go back to school
a few days early, please?"*

An Inconvenient Truth

"Adults are people, too."
They tell us this over and over again.

But it's one thing to hear it
after a heated argument with your
normally level headed parents

And another to have to watch a room full of
Super macho rugby players openly weep
over their dead friend.

Call Waiting

I call your phone every day
Mom hasn't gotten around
to calling the phone company yet
I wait patiently while the line trills
I get your voicemail every time.

Except on a random afternoon
After a grueling day at school
My stomach dropped
When instead of your voice

I heard

We're sorry
But the number
you have reached
is no longer in service

Please check the number in your directory
and try your call again.

Mount Comfort

What do you wear
to a cemetery

On a beautiful spring day
To sit in the lush green grass

And talk to a plaque
in the ground?

The Dress Rehearsal

"If you don't get the lead role it's their loss, Mary!
You are the brightest star in the sky.
If they can't recognize your talent,
I will go to the school
And quit the drama club on your behalf."

Dad,
I got the lead.
I wish you could be here
For opening night.

Maybe,
you'll be here in spirit.

Charlie's Song

The silence of the house
Is interrupted by
a gentle tune
From the laundry room
my dad is singing to our dog
A song he made up on the spot
just for Charlie

I hear it on some days
When Charlie waits for him
by the laundry room door

Wind Up Toy

How do I get out of bed each day?
Thanks for asking!
Why, you see,
I'm a classic wind-up toy!

Every morning
I gather up every inch
of my tangled web of grief and despair
and wrap it all up so tightly

That it propels me forward
For just enough time
Until it's time for bed again

My Saturday Plans

Actually, I can't make it to the movies on Saturday
I have to go to this rugby tournament for my dad

No, he's not playing
It's his memorial tournament
And I have to give a speech

You know what, never mind.
I'll talk to you later.

The Ballad of Allen Iverson

If I squint I can still see us
Sitting right there at the kitchen table

He holds the paper in his left hand
and uses his pencil to follow along the page
Because his reading glasses are, once again,
Sitting on top of his head

"A B+ in art?!"
"Dad, I told you I'm not good at art!"
"I know you told me that," he grumbles
Searching his head for the perfect
Metaphor or maybe even simile
"I got it! Do you know who
Allen Iverson is?"

My response poured out of my mouth
"No... But what does he
Have to do with my B+ in art...?"
I end my question early
He was already off to the races
A new internet tab open
YouTube
He types "Allen Iverson", "press conference", "practice"
Into the search bar

I sat and watched this gaggle of journalists
Press and pry about the PRACTICE Allen skipped
Instead of anything about the GAME he just played

I nodded my head
As my dad's eyes lit up

Finally,
He turns to me and says
"I know it's hard,
But, remember,
we're talking about practice."

Telephone

The never-ending
game of telephone
Humbles us all

Piece by piece
I recreate that day
To fill in my own gaps
Sometimes my wires
get crossed

Unfortunately, I think I've hit
a dead end

Ouija, Are You There?

I felt the planchette move!
I swear!
And, no,
(It wasn't Maddie).

I can't describe it
 We were moving along the board
Together
Two objects being acted upon

Whoever or whatever
 was with us that day
Said they were you
We weren't sure

 (It didn't feel right).

Mixtape

My mom had me go through all the boxes
And pick out what I want to keep
I have no idea how many CDs my dad even had
every genre
every color of the rainbow

Suddenly,
exploding iridescent flecks of light
catch my eye
Looks like Dad
made me a mixtape

I pop the disc into
The beat-up Ford I drive to school
I hear the guitar whine
as Dr. Dre's voice booms

Monster Protocol

Every night before bed
We would review the protocol
In the event
I were to encounter any monsters
Underneath my bed
I was instructed to inform you at once
So, you could intervene at once
And slay the beast

Your exact words
As I recall were
I will rip its head off

 I never found a monster under my bed
But some days
I have an invincible Hydra
Ravaging my mind
The heads keep growing
What do I do?

Untitled Conversation with a Complete Stranger at a Bonfire in the Middle of An Empty Field

"I don't know how you handle it every day!
I don't even know what I'd do if
My dad died!"

I look down at the sweating can
of Natural Light from a cooler
Dragged out here by a boy
Who may give me the time of day
If I keep a handle on my temper
And don't bring up anything
About my dead dad

"Somehow I manage."
I say almost as soft as a whisper
By the time
I light my new cigarette
My new companion is gone
I'm all alone
Again.

Player Stats: An Overview

My dad was not my coach
He just stood down
by the opposing team's goal
to give me real-time feedback
and tell me that I need to
step my game up.
Even after my fourth goal
and third assist.

He never used to
but now he misses every game.

Graduation (High School)

I waited until the last minute
To go to the mall to buy my dress
Everyone said we had to wear white
Because it's tradition

But no one knew where the tradition originated
I decorated my cap
Put on my gown and walked across the stage
We took photos
Had a party

 A few weeks later
I brought the diploma to the cemetery
To show you

Journal Prompt: How do you stay connected to your loved ones here on Earth and those who have passed? What helps you stay grounded in community?

_____

_____

_____

_____

_____

_____

_____

_____

_____

_____

_____

_____

_____

Part 2: Grief in Early 20s

First Date

My dad works in landscaping
I tell him
It's been 5 years
I think it's time for a little humor

and why do I need to
open up my deepest wound
on a first date
With a shy but nice enough guy
ho I'm never gonna see again?

Wales Vs. Australia

The guys came into town
For the World Cup
England is hosting, remember?

They had an extra ticket to the game
I tagged along
We sat right by the try line
Cheering and clinking bottles of Heineken

 At dinner
We couldn't help but talk about you
I will never forget
When each of them looked at me
with tear-filled eyes
And reminded me
How you left a larger-than-life
Hole in all our hearts

Daddy Issues

I wish I had
a better answer
When someone asks
So, how did your dad fuck your life up?
And I say
He died when I was 13.

An Ode to Father's Day

I never mark down
the day in my calendar
Trust me,
I really don't need the reminder

I don't count down the days
I don't browse the supermarket aisles
For the perfect greeting card
I don't make brunch reservations
Or plan a special golf outing

Most years I post another old photo
With the same flowery caption
As I try not
To drink the day away

Cheers!
To Father's Day!

Déjà Vu
"I don't know if I've told you this before…"

My eyes glaze over
I know the line by heart
Maybe they have told me before
Or maybe I just know it because
I hear it every fucking day

*"You know, on days like today, I really miss your
dad."*

Graduation (Undergrad)

They handed us two diplomas
One for each school system
I thought about your diploma
Hanging on the wall of your home office

We had a joint graduation party
with my closest friends
The plans almost fell through
But at the last possible moment
Everything worked out just fine

 It wasn't until later in the night
When everyone started to get all sentimental
And remind me
Just how proud you would have been of me

The knife cuts deeper each time

 We drank, we danced
We were merry
 Trust me
You would have been the life of the party

Journal Prompt: What helps you feel connected to others in your life. What is the easiest way for you to communicate with loved ones? You can list all the different ways you like to communicate verbally, non verbally, digitally, in person, etc.

_____

_____

_____

_____

_____

_____

_____

_____

_____

_____

_____

_____

_____

Part 3: Grief in Mid 20s

Missing Signal

I want to get my hearing checked
I think my left ear is the problem
Maybe something is stuck in it?

I'm not sure what
but the other day
I swore I heard my dad's voice
Out in the backyard

But it was so faint
and kept getting fainter
until I couldn't hear it at all.

Grief Journaling

I'm sick and tired
of being sick and tired
I drag myself through life
One day to another
Time lurches on
Floating between grief and memories
Misery and daydream

Coming Out (pt. 1)

Dad,

I'm gay.

Mom knows.

Everyone knows, actually.
I posted it on Facebook.

Well I didn't know what to write
Or how to come out
So, I just shared a photo of me and the girl
I'm dating
She's amazing and beautiful
And everything I've been looking for in this world.

I was never scared you and Mom wouldn't accept
me
I think that I was just lost for a long time
For many reasons
But I feel myself finding my way

I'll bring her by to meet you soon.

Graduation (Grad School)

They waived the requirement that we had to
Remain in the UK for the remainder of the program
The university closed all in-person activities
And I couldn't find the strength to try and wait out
A global pandemic
 I came home in May
Well, not back Home

 Mom lives in Pennsylvania

For the celebration
My friends and I got on Zoom
(it's a video chat application, like Skype)
And pretended to share a round of Famous Grouse
and ginger ale
In our local pub

 They said they'll mail me my degree
I had to update my address on file
Because I live with my girlfriend now
Mom and I weren't getting along
So, we found a practical solution

I still don't know if I'll be able to find a job
But I'm proud of myself for seeing this through until
the end

D.D.C.*

Is this your first meeting?

Don't worry!
We don't bite!

We just cry about
Our dead dads.

*The Dead Dad Club is a club for all individuals with a dead dad.

Health Update (2021)

We're not sure
what started it all
It may be impossible
to fully untangle the web

One day
I woke up in a foreign body
disconnected
distant
Off-kilter

 They say I have to reduce my stress
But how can you relax
when you no longer stood on solid ground?

Every day is so drastically different from the next
Crushing pain that takes away
All the life in your eyes
After some coaxing
They gave me a referral to a neurologist

Rehearsal Dinner

We didn't have a traditional rehearsal
Or even rehearsal dinner
Maddie, Mom, and I practiced walking down the aisle
Bailey and Deb did the same
Our friends practiced their speeches
Then, we ordered pizza
and sat by the camp fire

Friends and family are arriving from all over
as we speak
So, we wanted something easy-going
Before the Big Day

I haven't told Mom yet
That we put "Lovely Day" on the pre ceremony playlist
I will try to pull her aside tomorrow
To give her a heads up

Her dress fits me perfectly
The seamstress had to remove the original
Backing of the dress and replace it
With a brand new corset
Something borrowed something new
My friends will have to lace me up in the morning

We have a table for you
and Rob Roy
Where people can come up
And light a candle

For you
and anyone else
That couldn't be with us today

Hospital (Night One)

They took me up to the ward in the dead of night
I'm not sure why
We arrived at the ER in the early evening
They kept me in the first room for a long time
And said something about waiting for a bed

Hours later
 they finally took me up to the floor
The ward was dark

 We finished my intake
Then the nurse led me to my room
I tried calm my nerves
But I couldn't catch my breath

We arrived at my room
There were daffodils on the door
Your favorite flower

That was enough
to relax my tightening chest
And welcome the healing power of oxygen

Putting Pen to Paper

They gave me a notebook
When they came in the first morning
To drop off my change of clothes and toiletries
The nurse said I can use it during group therapy
or on my own
apparently journaling really helps some people

I picked up the ballpoint pen
And wrote and wrote and wrote
And wrote and wrote and wrote
Until my eyes grew weary
And my hand began to cramp
The words kept flowing out of me

Something was set free
Now it's all come bubbling to the surface

I'm going to show Bailey
Some of the poems
When she comes to visit later this week
I wrote one for you
I'll have to share it
When it's ready

For I think it
Could use a few more verses

Daffodils

On a gloomy morning
I stumbled down an uneven path
As I turned my head
I saw daffodils
And thought of you
Your smile, your laugh
How deeply I missed you
It brought me to tears
Knowing you were walking alongside me

On a misty afternoon
I awoke from a nap on a bus
As I looked out the foggy window
I saw daffodils
And I thought of you
Your bravery, your love for life
How deeply I wish you were beside me
I remembered how much time has passed
But I felt you sitting right there next to me

On a terrifying night
I walked down a dimly-lit hallway
As I arrived at my empty room
I saw daffodils on my door
And I thought of you
Your love for me, for all of us
How much in that moment I needed you
I stepped forward
And felt you hold out your hand
To remind me that you are always there

PNES*

Dad.
I had a seizure last night.

I don't know why.
All the sudden
I couldn't breathe
Before everything went black
I called out for you

I guess it lasted only a few minutes
They said they need to run more tests.

*Psychogenic Nonepileptic Seizures (PNES) are
non-epileptic seizure episodes that closely resemble
epileptic seizures are not caused by abnormal electri-
cal activity in the brain.

Journal Prompt: What are your favorite activities to do to help you relax when you are in distress? What you like about those activities? Why do you think these activities help you relax and ground yourself?

_____

_____

_____

_____

_____

_____

_____

_____

_____

_____

_____

_____

_____

Part 4: Grief in Late 20s

Coming Out (pt. 2)

Dad,

I think you got your wish after all
Because I'm definitely not a girl
I don't think I'm a boy either

I don't know if can even put it
Into words I can even understand
But the more I travel around the world
and all the people I meet
keeping telling me more and more
About how people like me who have
Always felt out of place all their lives
Have a home
A chosen home

Somewhere in between the binaries
and have been since the beginning of time!

Nothing changes the fact that
I'm still your oldest child
Just a more realized version

If anything you have helped
Put all of this in motion
I mean remember how
You defied gendered expectations of you
All the time

Your love of disco
Of art, of fashion, of movies
You've been surrounded by trans people
All along

We're just in full view now!

I know you understand.

Maybe I needed this monologue.
More than you did.

Your Valentine

I got the message from Mom
While sitting at my desk at work
We knew Nonnie's health was bad
We didn't know how quickly
The horrible monster would take over
And suck every last drop of life
From her frail frame

I debated whether or not
To call Auntie
So that I could say goodbye
Over the phone

She couldn't talk or open her eyes
I kept telling myself
That I never got to say goodbye to you
And I turned out fine

And then I remembered
That I didn't

Cousin said even though the timing was morbid
Maybe Nonnie was destined
To be your valentine this year

California (Night One)

I'm worried that
if I like it here too much
I may never go back
How will I go visit you
If I can't stomach getting on a plane?

Cross country driving
Seems ok
But we were so scared to stop
For gas or to use the bathroom
On the trip here
We tried our best to put on brave faces
But, we don't have anything small
Like a taser or a pocket knife
In case some jackass tries to hurt Bailey

I never thought
I'd get pushed so far out of home
By people who don't care
If we all live or die

I think you would like it here
We are a block from the beach
Mom is coming to visit soon
Maybe you can make your way over
As well

The Novel

I sat down one day
and began to write a story
About a kid just like me
and a father just like you
Torn apart by the universe
Too soon

I poured my memories
onto the pages
and filled in the gaps
With magic

The ending isn't a twist
But a reminder
That grief and memories never fade

Words of Wisdom

From a very young age
My dad always told me
"Mary, not everyone is going to like you
And that's ok!"

For many years
I obsessed over how to make myself
More agreeable
Palatable
So no one had the excuse
Not to like me

Turns out,
I may have missed his lesson entirely.
Because after a few more years
Reflecting on his words
I discovered that
I could actually just exist fully as myself
and not give a fuck.

Health Update (2025)

They said they found adhesions
More than the last time

I've asked the doctor about
A hysterectomy and she said
an oophorectomy would be a good idea too
Without hesitation
I choose myself
But I still weep for what could've been

I would loved to sit in the backyard
With you and your grandchild
I think we'd have much to discuss
like

Letting go
         and
                Accepting the things we cannot
change.

Fatherless Behavior

Everything you do
is technically fatherless behavior
She chuckles

The joke lands on
My shoulder like
a gentle monarch butterfly

But the punchline
is a swift punch to the gut

I Hate This Poem

Writing this chapbook sucks.
Every breakthrough
is followed by a breakdown

My childhood memories
are in disarray
scattered across the floor

Does picking the meat off the bones
Of my own grief
really count as healing?

Pacing

I want to keep going
Shrug it off
I've dealt with worse before
I should be able to push through,

Then,

I remember
You drove yourself
to the hospital
after the pain had gotten so bad
You had already waited two days
You didn't want to worry us
You didn't think it was that serious

I don't blame you for what you didn't know
But it's important to remember
That we are meant to slow down sometimes
Our bodies are precious
our energy is precious
Right?

So,
I'm going to go sit down for a while.

Journal Prompt: Where is your safe space? You can describe a physical space (like a reading space) or an imagined space (your "happy place" you visit when meditating). What does that space offer you? How can you incorporate safety into other spaces in your life?

_____

_____

_____

_____

_____

_____

_____

_____

_____

_____

_____

_____

_____

Epilogue

At the end of the day all we have is community. I recommend identifying all the different types of relationships you have in your life-- romantic, platonic, strong, casual, seasonal-- and think about how you can sustain those bonds. We need to practice asking for and receiving care from others before we can sustainably provide care to others. I understand that in emergencies, especially caused by complex trauma, we are stuck in fight, fight, freeze, fawn and want to feel safe. You will feel safe when you invest in community and trust. I trust my friends to recommend restaurants to me. I also can trust that my friends will hold me when I'm sad and sit with me when I need to slow down.

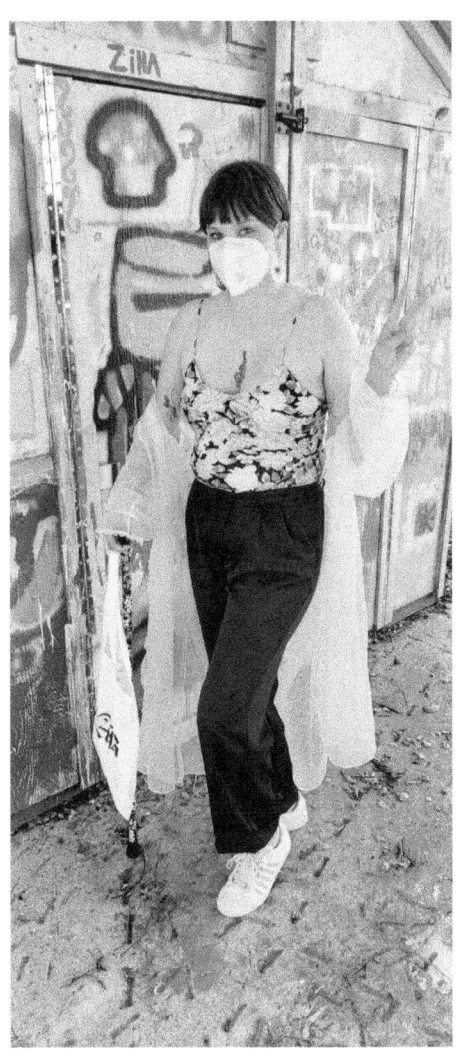

M.K. Sullivan is a queer, disabled poet who writes about grief, trauma, alienation, and how we can come together to care for one another. Based in Southern California but raised in the Southeastern U.S., their writing is rooted in a disability justice politic to elevate biting critiques of ableism and patriarchy.

Publisher's Note

Daxson publishing was created to help marginalized artists and their allies publish their work, so the world can hear their voice. The vision for this publishing house is to help people get their work out there, and not have them struggle finding their way through the publishing process. Everyone's voice deserves to be heard, and we are here to help. If you are interested in submitting a manuscript, email daxsonpublishing@gmail.com.

Support our cause! Buy our books at daxsonpublishing. com.

www.ingramcontent.com/pod-product-compliance
Lightning Source LLC
Chambersburg PA
CBHW071538120626
46550CB00006B/2502